AMERICAN HISTORY COMIC BOOKS

12 Reproducible Comic Books With Activities Guaranteed
to Get Kids Excited About Key Events and People
in American History

by Joseph D'Agnese & Jack Silbert

NEW YORK • TORONTO • LONDON • AUCKLAND • SYDNEY
MEXICO CITY • NEW DELHI • HONG KONG • BUENOS AIRES

Teaching
Resources

Cover design by Maria Lilja
Interior design by Russell Bart
Illustrations by Mark Zingarelli

ISBN 0-439-46605-9
Copyright © 2005 by Joseph D'Agnese and Jack Silbert
All rights reserved.
Printed in the U.S.A.

8 9 10   40   15 16 17 18 19 20/0

# CONTENTS

 # INTRODUCTION

Welcome to *American History Comic Books*! The star of these comic books—wacky, fearless (let's be honest, not *that* fearless) time traveler Scooter McGinty—has a love for history that your students will soon share. McGinty visits notable moments in American history, from the landing of the Pilgrims to the dawn of the Internet age. Students may have read dry accounts of these events in textbooks, but in this collection they will sail through history delivered in a lively comic-book format.

As far back as the 1940s, comic books have been used to educate while entertaining young readers. Generations of students learned the characters and plots of great literary works through adaptations in the *Classics Illustrated* comic-book series. Faced with information presented in this familiar format, the student's natural connection to the material aids in the learning process. (Comics can especially motivate otherwise hesitant male readers.)

In *American History Comic Books*, fun illustrations and humorous dialogue bring historical figures to life. Students stand beside Ben Franklin as he flies his famous kite, and sit on the horse with Paul Revere as he makes his famous ride. All the while, Scooter serves as a tour guide, asking many of the questions students may wonder themselves—when he's not getting himself into another zany mix-up!

After each adventure, Scooter will prompt students to answer five "Quick Quiz" questions on the material they've just covered. The questions cover reading comprehension, critical thinking, research, and writing prompts. At the end of this book, you'll find a detailed answer key.

How To Use These Comic Books

Scooter's travels are divided into 12 four-page comic books. Simply photocopy each four-page book for your class when you are ready to present that lesson. (To save paper—and to duplicate the comic-book experience more closely—use the double-sided feature in your copy machine, if available.) Staple the comics in the upper left-hand corner and distribute them to students.

Presentation Strategies

You can use the American history comics in a variety of ways: as homework, as extra credit after a test, or as a substitute-teaching tool. The portability of the comics makes them a perfect take-home assignment. But for the most impact, use them as part of an in-class unit on one of the historical topics. This book's additional sections will help you do just that.

Background Notes and Teaching Ideas

Immediately following this introduction, we've provided you with a section entitled "Background Notes and Teaching Ideas." The notes give you a context for each comic by explaining the historic events that preceded those your students are about to read. Read this background information for your own benefit, and if you wish, read it to your students prior to distributing the comics. Even before this, you may wish to have a class discussion, asking students what they already know about the topic to be covered.

For a lively class activity when presenting a comic book, have students read aloud the different characters' dialogue, with narrators handling the captions and "Fact Boxes."

The Teaching Ideas are primarily intended for use after the comic has been read and the Quick Quiz questions have been answered. These ideas will provide you with additional discussion topics, cross-curricular extension activities, and general suggestions to help you connect the material to students' everyday lives.

The Web Links feature official Web sites for each topic covered in the book. In an effort to provide reliable information, we've chosen sites operated by American museums, the U.S. government, and nonprofit organizations wherever possible.

In the back of the book, you'll find a Historical Who's Who that gives a succinct, alphabetized list of all the major real-life characters mentioned in the comic books. For each individual, we provide the dates in history when the person lived, as well as a brief biographical description of his or her contribution. Use this section for your own reference, to generate additional quiz questions or a matching activity, or simply to photocopy for your students.

History is an important and vital subject. Understanding the twists and turns of time can help students place current events into a recognizable framework. Remember: While it's always nice to have a guide like Scooter McGinty to help students navigate unfamiliar eras, it is more important to have a teacher like you leading the way. So, if you're ready, join Scooter as we go...to the time machine!

—Joseph D'Agnese & Jack Silbert

BACKGROUND NOTES AND TEACHING IDEAS

THE PILGRIMS OF PLYMOUTH

Beginning with Christopher Columbus in 1492, various European explorers reached the "New World," including Amerigo Vespucci, Giovanni da Verrazano, Jacques Cartier, Hernando de Soto, Francisco Vásquez de Coronado, Juan Ponce de León, Henry Hudson, Sir Francis Drake, and Sir Walter Raleigh. Spain, France, Holland, and England began to establish colonies for commercial ventures. Jamestown, founded in 1607 in what is now Virginia, was England's first permanent colony.

The colonization story that continues to captivate the American imagination is that of the Pilgrims—the first people to come for freedom, rather than riches. In the 1530s, because of disagreements with the Pope, King Henry VIII banished the Catholic Church from Britain, replacing it with the Church of England with him at its head. At that time, a group of people wanted even more change; they didn't want *any* church officials. Many were imprisoned for their beliefs. In 1620, about a hundred of these separatists, or pilgrims, decided to sever ties with Europe and head for America.

Teaching Ideas: This comic is best used seasonally, around Thanksgiving. Before reading the comic, ask students to share what they know about the holiday and its historic origins. After reading the comic, ask them what facts surprised them. As a multicurricular extension activity, have students write and perform their own Thanksgiving play, culminating in a Thanksgiving "feast." Invite them to bring in food that represents their own ethnic heritage.

Web Link: www.teacher.scholastic.com/thanksgiving

This Scholastic site describes the Pilgrims' experience from the *Mayflower* to the first Thanksgiving and offers a concise teacher's guide.

THE BOSTON TEA PARTY

England always saw the American colonies as a money-making venture. Colonists needed British goods, and trade with them generated important raw goods and income for businesses back in England. Whenever Britain found itself in a tight spot financially, it cast a greedy eye toward the colonies—and tension was the inevitable result.

Beginning in the 1730s, many colonists believed that they should have a say in their government. However, little thought was given to independence, as the British protected the colonies from the French and Indians. Between 1689 and 1763, England fought four wars with France for control of North America, the Indians often fighting on the side of the French. But when the warring ended in 1763, the colonists felt betrayed as Britain handed over all lands west of the Appalachian Mountains to the Indians. The colonists felt the land they had fought for was rightfully theirs, and tension with England continued to grow.

Teaching Ideas: To help bring the concept of "taxation without representation" home to students, ask them to imagine that the school cafeteria has decided to double the price of school lunch. Students ask to have a say in the menu selection, but that request is denied. It is also decided that outside food is not allowed to be eaten on school grounds. How would they feel? What steps would they take to make their grievances known?

Web Link: www.pbs.org/ktca/liberty/chronicle_boston1774.html

From the site for the PBS series "Liberty! The American Revolution," this fictional newspaper article describes the Boston Tea Party and its causes, with links to related topics.

MIDNIGHT RIDE OF PAUL REVERE!

At the end of our Boston Tea Party comic, Scooter McGinty says that as a result of destroying the tea in Boston Harbor, "The King will be angry, and the Colonies will come under even harsher rule." This harsher rule took the form of the Intolerable Acts: no ships could enter the harbor until the tea was paid for; the Massachusetts colonial government was shut down; and thousands of British soldiers were sent to Boston and housed in the homes of local citizens.

In 1774, colonial leaders (including George Washington, Patrick Henry, Samuel Adams, and John Adams) gathered at the First Continental Congress to plan a response to the Intolerable Acts. Some argued for a total separation from England, though most hoped for a peaceful settlement. They did make it clear that the colonies wished to control their own affairs.

England refused to heed these requests. As a result, the boycott of British products spread, militias of armed minutemen began to form around Concord, Massachusetts, and colonists braced themselves for war. On April 18, 1775—the night our comic takes place—3,500 troops were sent by the British to confiscate arms from the minutemen.

Teaching Ideas: Paul Revere required a horse, a boat, two additional riders, and a prearranged signal to deliver a message a mere 19 miles from Boston to Concord. Have students think about how technology has altered this situation! What options do they have to deliver a similar message today?

Web Link: www.paulreverehouse.org

This site, operated by the Paul Revere Memorial Association, provides a biography, a detailed account of Revere's midnight ride, and information on his historic homestead.

THE SHOCKING LIFE OF BENJAMIN FRANKLIN

Franklin was born in Boston in 1706, the son of a poor candle maker. At age 12, he was apprenticed to his brother James, a printer. But at age 17, Benjamin struck out on his own, running away to Philadelphia, the city that he would be identified with in history. We have singled him out in this

collection because he symbolizes the wit and wisdom of early America. Franklin was one of the nation's first Renaissance men—an expert in science, literature, politics, and more.

Teaching Ideas: Students can make electricity themselves, without standing in a rainstorm! Ask them to inflate a balloon and simply rub it against their sweater or hair. The balloon will stick to a wall. Why? Students have created static electricity. When they rubbed the balloon, it picked up extra negatively charged electrons, which are attracted to the positively charged electrons in the wall.

Web Link: www.ushistory.org/franklin

This site contains everything you ever wanted to know about Franklin, including a comprehensive list of his famous sayings.

THE CONSTITUTION AND THE BILL OF RIGHTS

General Lord Cornwallis, the British commander in the South, surrendered to General George Washington on October 19, 1781. Meanwhile, in England, Parliament had grown frustrated with the expensive war. Peace talks began in April 1782 and a treaty was signed in Paris on September 3, 1783, giving the former colonies all land east of the Mississippi River. With the war over, the former colonies had to create a new government.

Teaching Ideas: The preamble to the Constitution begins with "We the people." But who were those people? At the time the Constitution was ratified, African Americans were excluded from voting, as were women, and in many areas, white men who were not property owners. Invite students to discuss the importance of the amendments to the Constitution, which granted rights to these Americans. Ask: Are there still groups of people who are not fully included in "We the people"?

Web Link: www.archives.gov/national_archives_experience/charters/constitution.html

From the National Archives, this site offers the full text of both the U.S. Constitution and the Bill of Rights, as well as biographies of the signers of the Constitution.

THE LEWIS & CLARK EXPEDITION

In the beginning of the 19th century France was at war with England, and the new French emperor Napoléon Bonaparte badly needed funds for this effort. At the time, France still owned a vast parcel of land in North America, stretching north from the Gulf of Mexico, west of the Mississippi River, and all the way to the Rocky Mountains. In 1803, President Thomas Jefferson sent diplomats James Monroe and Robert Livingston to France to meet with Napoleon. An agreement was made, and France's Louisiana Territory was sold to the U.S. for $15 million. The Louisiana Purchase instantly doubled the size of the young nation.

Teaching Ideas: Ask students to research the history of your state. Was it part of the original 13 colonies, part of the Louisiana Purchase, or acquired later? What Native American tribe(s) inhabited the territories that became your state? Which explorers first reached your area? What did they find?

Web Link: www.lewisandclark200.org

This site was created for the bicentennial celebration (2003–2006) of the Lewis and Clark expedition.

CALIFORNIA GOLD RUSH!

California is still influenced by its Spanish ancestry today. From 1769 to 1821, California was a colonial province of the Spanish empire. In 1821, California came under Mexican rule, after Mexico gained independence from Spain. The prosperous territory was only transferred to the United States following the U.S.–Mexican War. After a brief period as an independent state, California was admitted to the Union in 1850. Notice that statehood came shortly after the discovery of gold!

Teaching Ideas: The world's fascination with gold continues to this day. We honor athletes with gold medals, we present loved ones with gold jewelry, and the word *gold* has become synonymous with high value. Our U.S. currency was for a long time guaranteed by gold held by the federal government. That means that for every dollar in circulation, there was $1 worth of gold owned by the government. Ask students to research the history of the "gold standard" and the national gold repository, Fort Knox. Students could also look up the current value of gold.

Web Link: www.sfmuseum.org/hist1/index0.1.html#gold

A thorough online exhibit presented by the Museum of the City of San Francisco, this site includes many firsthand accounts of the Gold Rush.

THE STORY OF AMERICA'S IMMIGRANTS

England, Ireland, and Germany had a long tradition of emigration to the United States. In the late 19th century, they were joined by eastern and southern Europeans, who began to come in large numbers. Like America's first European settlers (see background notes for "The Pilgrims of Plymouth," page 6), some came for freedom, while others came for opportunity. Russian Jews fled *pogroms*, raids by Russian soldiers who robbed and murdered them. Italian and Polish farmers came because they were losing their land to more powerful property owners. While the United States received the lion's share of immigrants, other regions such as Australia, Canada, and South America became popular destinations as well. Immigration is still a worldwide issue. The global economy has encouraged people to seek employment opportunities in nations where their skills are in great demand. Social and political unrest around the world still causes people to flee persecution and unacceptable living conditions in their homelands.

Teaching Ideas: Hold an international fair in your classroom. Have students research the customs and traditions of their ancestors and bring in examples of traditional artwork, crafts, clothing, foods, music, dances, and so on. Challenge them to find and discuss the similarities in the various cultures.

Web Links: www.nps.gov/stli/prod02.htm

In addition to history, the National Park Service's Statue of Liberty site lists fun statistics and the full text of Emma Lazarus's poem "The New Colossus."

www.ellisisland.org

At the Statue of Liberty–Ellis Island Foundation site, students can type in their last names and find out which of their ancestors passed through Ellis Island.

HENRY FORD AND THE ASSEMBLY LINE

Like many inventions, the automobile is not the product of a single person. Rather, it was developed over a period of more than a hundred years. In 1769, French engineer Nicolas Joseph Cugnot invented the first self-propelling vehicle, a steam-driven tractor. Others, such as Scotsman Robert Anderson in the 1830s, built early electric vehicles. But it was the gasoline engine, perfected by Germans Gottlieb Daimler (in 1885) and Karl Benz (in 1886), that paved the way for the modern automobile.

Stress to students that Henry Ford by no means invented the automobile. But his contributions to the production process were a critical link in the chain. Ford was born in 1863 near Dearborn, Michigan, to a prosperous farming family. From an early age, Henry disliked farm work and instead tinkered with machines. At age 16 he left home for Detroit, where he found work as an apprentice machinist. He worked his way to chief engineer of the Edison Illuminating Company, and in his spare time began to work on a vehicle he would call the Quadricycle.

Teaching Ideas: To examine the efficiency of the assembly line process, divide the class into two competing "companies." Explain that they will attempt to build as many identical copies of an object as possible. The object could be anything (for example, paper airplane, greeting card, or paper hat). The only criteria is that the manufacturing process should involve several easily performed steps: cutting the paper, folding, taping, stapling, marking with a company logo, and so on. Each company should have the identical number of resources: paper, scissors, tape, markers, and so on. But one company will use an assembly line with each person performing only one task; the other company will have each employee create the object on his or her own, sharing tools and resources with their fellow employees. Set a time limit and see which company produces the most objects. Afterwards, discuss the pros and cons of each system. Which system produced more? In which system were the objects most identical?

Web Link: www.hfmgv.org/exhibits/hf

The Henry Ford Museum's site features an online exhibit on the life of Henry Ford and a history of the Ford Motor Company.

THE FIGHT FOR WOMEN'S RIGHTS

The history of women's rights in the U.S. stretches from the dawn of the republic to modern time. As stated in the Teaching Ideas for "The Constitution and the Bill of Rights" (page 8), a number of important groups were seemingly excluded by these original documents. Since then, activists from all walks of life have persuaded Congress to rectify these inequalities. Even before the Constitution, powerful women tried to get their views recognized. When John Adams was working on the Declaration of Independence at the Second Continental Congress, his wife Abigail wrote, asking that he and the other men "remember the ladies."

Well into the 19th century most Americans held stereotypical views about the domestic roles of men and women. Still, individual voices began to be heard. Speakers such as Frances Wright and Sarah Grimké traveled the country, advocating women's rights. Their voices struck a chord with some families, who sent their daughters to new schools for women. In 1833, Oberlin College became the first coeducational university in the U.S. Other schools, such as Mount Holyoke, Vassar, Smith, and Wellesley, opened exclusively for women. In 1840, the World Anti-Slavery Convention was held in London. Elizabeth Cady Stanton and Lucretia Mott tried to attend, but were refused entry. This insult inspired them to hold the first Women's Rights Convention, where our story begins.

Teaching Ideas: As a prereading activity, ask students to discuss any differences they notice between the way society treats men and women. After students have read the comic, give them a take-home assignment: Interview an older female family member and ask her about how men and women were treated. What changes have the interviewees noticed in their lifetimes?

Web Link: www.nmwh.org

The National Women's History Museum offers a step-by-step history of the suffrage movement and images of artifacts from the period.

AMERICA'S RACE TO THE MOON

The first real steps toward space flight came in the 1930s and '40s, when German scientists experimented with long-range rockets. After World War II, U.S. and Soviet governments put some of these scientists to work. The unexpected launch of *Sputnik* was regarded by the U.S. as another dangerous move in the "Cold War" by the Soviet Union, America's new enemy.

The Cold War was a long period of hostility. Although there were never any direct military attacks, both sides were always in conflict with each other, each trying to gain the upper hand. The rise and spread of Soviet Communism seemed like a direct threat to American democracy and to our way of life. Any U.S. citizen suspected of Communist sympathies was treated as a criminal or shunned by neighbors. Meanwhile, the "arms race"—the stockpiling of nuclear weapons by both sides—greatly heightened the tension. As our comic begins, the nation is poised to begin the "space race."

Teaching Ideas: Have students investigate early fictional accounts of space flight and journeys to the moon, such as *From the Earth to the Moon* (1865) and *Round the Moon* (1870) by Jules Verne, and *The First Men in the Moon* (1901) by H.G. Wells. How do the science-fiction tales stack up against what really happened?

Web Link: history.nasa.gov

The National Aeronautics and Space Administration provides histories of all their missions, technical data on all the crafts, and biographies of the astronauts.

COMPUTERS AND THE INTERNET

The development of mechanical devices to aid in counting and calculating stretches back to ancient times. Modern calculators and computers can trace their real roots to the 17th century. In 1623, Germany's Wilhelm Schickard built the first mechanical calculator, which worked with six digits. In 1642, the French mathematician Blaise Pascal built a calculator with gears and dials that could handle eight digits. In 1694, German mathematician Gottfried Wilhelm von Leibniz improved Pascal's design, building a calculator that could multiply.

In 1820, Charles Xavier Thomas de Colmar of France built the arithometer, an office machine capable of adding, subtracting, multiplying, and dividing. His machine was widely used until World War I. Also in the early 1820s, England's Charles Babbage began to design a massive, steam-powered machine he called the Difference Engine, which would calculate and print astronomical tables. The project was never completed, but Babbage moved on to another machine, which he called the Analytical Engine. As conceived, it would use punch cards and be able to solve any mathematical problem. The Countess of Lovelace, Augusta Ada Byron, worked with Babbage and wrote a famous thorough description of the Analytical Engine. She is considered the world's first female computer programmer. In 1889, American Herman Hollerith used a similar punch-card system to compute the U.S. census results. His company later became IBM. The use of punch cards lasted well into the 20th century.

Teaching Ideas: Computers have developed so rapidly that your students may not be able to conceive of life without them. Share your experiences with calculators and computers in your lifetime. What changes have you witnessed? Now ask your students to describe changes they have seen in home computers, video-game systems, and home entertainment.

Web Link: www.computerhistory.org

The Computer History Museum salutes the information age.

SCOOTER'S QUICK QUIZ

1. What was the "Mayflower Compact"?

2. Why couldn't Scooter find the famous Plymouth Rock?

3. What was the name of the first American Indian the Pilgrims encountered?

4. In the library or on the Internet, look up the stories of famous Pilgrims William Bradford and Myles Standish. Who were they, and what were their contributions to the Plymouth colony?

5. Research the history of Thanksgiving as a national holiday. How does your family celebrate that day?

SCOOTER'S QUICK QUIZ

1. What was the Stamp Act? What were the Townshend Acts?

2. What was the name of the group of citizens who led the Boston Tea Party?

3. Why were the colonists upset about the Tea Act?

4. To fight the taxes placed upon them, the colonists used an action called a "boycott." Look up this word. Can you find other historic boycotts?

5. The colonists were known to shout the phrase "No taxation without representation!" They didn't like being asked to pay more and more in taxes when they didn't have a representative in the British government. Why do you think this was so important to them? Who represents your views in the U.S. government?

SCOOTER'S QUICK QUIZ

1. What signal did Paul Revere use to alert the patriots whether the British were traveling by land or sea?

2. What important mission did Paul Revere need to accomplish in Lexington?

3. What were the names of the two patriots who joined Revere at Lexington?

4. Find Boston, Charlestown, Lexington, and Concord on a map of Massachusetts. What river did Revere have to cross to get to Charlestown from Boston?

5. Find and read the famous poem, "The Midnight Ride of Paul Revere" by Henry Wadsworth Longfellow. How is it different from the story you just read?

SCOOTER'S QUICK QUIZ

1. Why did Ben Franklin fly a kite in a storm? What was he trying to prove?

2. Who were the five men assigned to write the Declaration of Independence?

3. What was the name of Franklin's famous publication?

4. In the library or the Internet, look up some of Ben Franklin's famous sayings. Pick one and explain it in your own words.

5. Ben Franklin's face is on the $100 bill. Only one other person who was not a U.S. President is shown on a current U.S. bill. Research the name of that person and tell why you think he deserved this honor.

Scholastic Teaching Resources

TO WIN THE STATES' APPROVAL, TEN AMENDMENTS WERE FINALLY ADDED TO THE CONSTITUTION. MORE AMENDMENTS WOULD BE ADDED LATER IN AMERICAN HISTORY, BUT THE FIRST TEN WOULD ALWAYS BE CALLED THE "BILL OF RIGHTS."

HEAR YE! HEAR YE! THIS BILL OF RIGHTS GIVES YOU THE FREEDOM OF SPEECH, RELIGION, PRESS, TO ASSEMBLE PEACEFULLY, THE RIGHT TO BEAR ARMS, THE RIGHT TO A FAIR AND SPEEDY TRIAL BY JURY, FREEDOM FROM UNFAIR SEARCHES OF YOUR HOMES, THE RIGHT OF ALL STATES TO MAKE LAWS THAT HAVE NOT BEEN MADE BY CONGRESS--

NOW THAT THEY'VE ADDED THE BILL OF RIGHTS, I GIVE THE CONSTITUTION A THUMBS-UP! THE GOVERNMENT IS SHARING THE POWER WITH THE PEOPLE!

TO TEACH PEOPLE HOW IMPORTANT IT WAS FOR THEIR STATES TO APPROVE THE CONSTITUTION, JAMES MADISON, JOHN JAY, AND ALEXANDER HAMILTON PUBLISHED A SERIES OF ESSAYS CALLED "THE FEDERALIST PAPERS."

READ ALL ABOUT IT! A CENTRAL GOVERNMENT IS A GOOD GOVERNMENT!

THE GOVERNMENT HAS THE POWER--BUT SO DO THE PEOPLE!

WE ONLY NEED 9 STATES, BUT WE WANT EVERY STATE TO APPROVE THE CONSTITUTION!

FEDERALIST PAPER
CENTRAL GOVT.

FEDERALIST
PEOPLE POWER

FEDERALIST
APPROVE IT!

HEY, ALEXANDER HAMILTON! YOU'RE ON THE $10 BILL!

THE CONSTITUTION WAS RATIFIED, WITH NINE STATES' APPROVAL, ON JUNE 21, 1788. (THE REMAINING FOUR STATES LATER RATIFIED IT.) LESS THAN A YEAR LATER, THE EXECUTIVE BRANCH HELD A SPECIAL CEREMONY...

APRIL 30, 1789
IN THE NATION'S ORIGINAL CAPITAL-- NEW YORK CITY!

FROM THIS DAY FORWARD, YOU WILL BE CALLED HIS HIGHNESS, THE PRESIDENT OF THE UNITED STATES AND PROTECTOR OF THEIR LIBERTIES!

SOUNDS STUFFY, DOESN'T IT? I BELIEVE CONGRESS JUST WANTS ME TO BE KNOWN AS THE PRESIDENT OF THE UNITED STATES.

SCOOTER'S QUICK QUIZ

1. What was the name of the WEAK document used to govern the colonies during the Revolutionary War?

2. Who wrote much of the U.S. Constitution?

3. The three branches of government are often called a system of "checks and balances." What do you think this means? What is being checked, and what is balanced?

4. Dividing Congress into two houses was known as the Great Compromise. Research why the Convention delegates did this.

5. Look up the Bill of Rights and choose one amendment to explain to your classmates. What freedoms does it guarantee us?

Scholastic Teaching Resources

SCOOTER'S QUICK QUIZ

1. What was the new land that Lewis & Clark were asked to explore?

2. What was the name of their brave group of explorers?

3. List three ways that Indians helped Lewis & Clark along the way.

4. What were the three things President Jefferson asked them to do on their travels? Can you describe some of the ways they accomplished these tasks?

5. If you could explore an unknown place, what would you bring with you and what would you want to study along the way?

SCOOTER'S QUICK QUIZ

1. Why were the miners called "Forty-Niners"?

2. Who was the U.S. President whose speech sparked the Gold Rush?

3. Marshall's fellow workers accused him of finding "fool's gold." Can you guess what that means? Look it up to check your ideas.

4. Some Forty-Niners from the East Coast didn't travel by land to California. They went by boat. Which do you think is faster--traveling by land or by sea?

5. If you found gold, what would you do? Would you act more like John Sutter or more like Sam Brannan?

FIRST, THE NEWCOMERS HAD TO BE PROCESSED. MORE THAN 12 MILLION PEOPLE PASSED THROUGH THE ELLIS ISLAND IMMIGRATION STATION IN NEW YORK HARBOR FROM 1892 TO 1954. IN A SINGLE DAY IN 1924, 11,747 IMMIGRANTS WERE PROCESSED THERE!

AT ELLIS ISLAND, CROWDED CONDITIONS AND TOUGH MEDICAL INSPECTIONS AWAITED IMMIGRANTS. SOME, WHO WERE FOUND TO BE PHYSICALLY OR MENTALLY UNFIT, WERE SENT RIGHT BACK TO EUROPE. AMONG THE IMMIGRANTS, ELLIS ISLAND WAS KNOWN AS THE "ISLAND OF TEARS."

HEY, CAN YOU HURRY IT UP, DOC? THEY NEED ME IN THE NEXT CARTOON PANEL.

CONDITIONS WERE NO BETTER IN THE CITIES. IMMIGRANT FAMILIES LIVED IN TINY APARTMENTS IN CHEAPLY MADE BUILDINGS CALLED TENEMENTS. STILL, MANY FOUND A SENSE OF COMMUNITY IN NEIGHBORHOODS FILLED WITH PEOPLE FROM THEIR HOME COUNTRIES. EVERYONE SPOKE THE SAME LANGUAGE AND ATE FAMILIAR FOODS IN THESE GHETTOS.

SONNY! GET YOUR 16 BROTHERS AND SISTERS UP HERE TO THIS ONE-ROOM APARTMENT BEFORE YOUR DINNER GETS COLD!

ON SECOND THOUGHT, MAYBE YOU SHOULDN'T COME OVER FOR SUPPER.

MARKET

THE IMMIGRANTS WERE A CHEAP LABOR SOURCE FOR MANY AMERICAN INDUSTRIES SUCH AS THE RAILROADS, STEEL MILLS, COAL MINES, MEAT-PACKING PLANTS AND CLOTHING MAKERS. MANY FACTORIES WERE KNOWN AS SWEATSHOPS BECAUSE OF THEIR LONG HOURS, LOW PAY, AND DANGEROUS CONDITIONS.

DO WE GET A COFFEE BREAK?

PEOPLE BORN IN AMERICA WERE NOT ALWAYS KIND TO THE NEWCOMERS. SOME WANTED THE IMMIGRANTS TO GIVE UP THE CUSTOMS OF THEIR HOME COUNTRIES. OTHERS THOUGHT THAT THEY SHOULD NOT BE ALLOWED IN THE UNITED STATES AT ALL.

YOU'RE NOT SMART! YOU'LL NEVER BE *REAL* AMERICANS!

LAWS PASSED IN 1921 AND 1924 CHANGED THE U.S. IMMIGRATION POLICY. THOSE FROM ENGLAND, IRELAND, AND GERMANY -- WHERE THE PARENTS OF MOST PEOPLE BORN IN AMERICA CAME FROM -- WERE ALLOWED IN. ALL OTHER IMMIGRATION WAS SEVERELY LIMITED UNTIL 1965.

AT THE SAME TIME, OTHER AMERICANS TRIED TO HELP THE IMMIGRANTS. IN CHICAGO, JANE ADDAMS HELPED IMMIGRANTS GET JOBS AND EDUCATE AND CARE FOR THEIR CHILDREN. IN NEW YORK, JACOB RIIS WORKED TO IMPROVE THE GHETTOS BY SHOWING HIS PHOTOGRAPHS OF THE BAD LIVING CONDITIONS.

THE IMMIGRANT EXPERIENCE HAS IMPROVED OVER TIME, BUT MANY NEWCOMERS TO THESE SHORES FACED SIMILAR HARDSHIPS. THE COMING TOGETHER OF DIFFERENT PEOPLES AND CULTURES IS WHAT AMERICA IS TRULY FAMOUS FOR. WE ARE A MELTING POT-- A NATION OF IMMIGRANTS!

SCOOTER'S QUICK QUIZ

1. What was the name of the place in New York where most immigrants were processed?

2. Which country gave us the Statue of Liberty and why? What has it come to represent?

3. Why do you think Jacob Riis's photographs changed the way people thought about immigrant life?

4. Research your own family's immigrant story. What nation were your ancestors from? Who was the first to come to the United States?

5. What are the benefits of a society that is a melting pot of many different cultures?

SCOOTER'S QUICK QUIZ

1. What was the name of the very first car that Henry Ford built?

2. Name two other cars that Henry Ford built. Based on these, can you figure out the system he used for naming cars?

3. Why did Henry Ford want to build an assembly line?

4. Henry Ford's "anti-Semitism" has hurt his historical image. Look up the word "anti-Semitism" and research the role it played in World War II.

5. Make a time line of important moments in automobile history. Report to the class on your favorite all-time automobile.

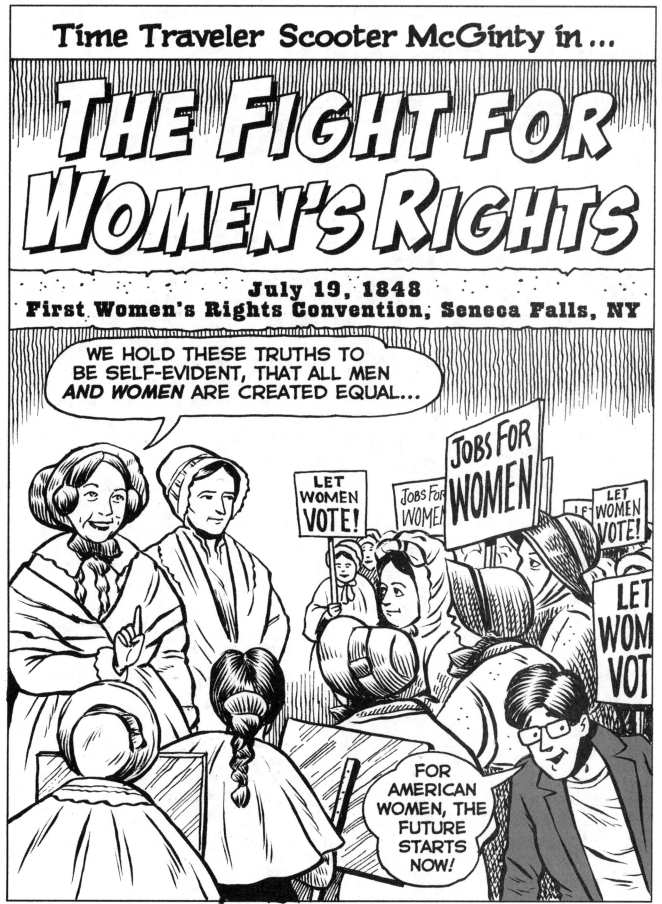

BUT THEY OPENED THE DOORS FOR SO MANY OTHER WOMEN WHO HAVE MADE THEIR MARK ON AMERICAN HISTORY. HERE ARE JUST A FEW OF THEM.

ELEANOR ROOSEVELT: FIRST LADY AND HUMANITARIAN

HATTIE WYATT CARAWAY OF ARKANSAS: 1ST WOMAN ELECTED U.S. SENATOR

ELLA GRASSO OF CONNECTICUT: 1ST WOMAN ELECTED GOVERNOR

ROSA PARKS: HERO OF THE CIVIL RIGHTS MOVEMENT

BETTY FRIEDAN: FOUNDER OF NATIONAL ORGANIZATION OF WOMEN

SANDRA DAY O'CONNOR AND RUTH BADER GINSBERG: 1ST AND 2ND FEMALE SUPREME COURT JUSTICES

GERALDINE FERRARO: 1ST FEMALE VICE-PRESIDENTIAL CANDIDATE

JANET RENO: 1ST FEMALE U.S. ATTORNEY GENERAL

MADELEINE ALBRIGHT: 1ST FEMALE U.S. SECRETARY OF STATE--HIGHEST RANKING WOMAN EVER IN U.S. GOVERNMENT

HEY MISTER! WHAT ABOUT ME?

UH...WHO ARE YOU?

I'M GOING TO BE THE FIRST FEMALE PRESIDENT OF THE UNITED STATES!

NOT TOO FAR INTO THE FUTURE, I HOPE! TO THE TIME MACHINE!

SCOOTER'S QUICK QUIZ

1. Who organized the first Women's Rights Convention and where was it held?

2. What is the link between the fight for slaves' rights and women's rights, as explained by Sojourner Truth?

3. Why do you think Susan B. Anthony cast a vote in Rochester, even though she knew it was against the law?

4. Research the life of one of the historic women in this comic. What are some of her achievements, and how has her work affected life in the United States?

5. Look up the Equal Rights Amendment, which Congress passed in 1972, but which never became national law. What rights are women still fighting for today?

Scholastic Teaching Resources

EVEN WITH SHEPARD'S FLIGHT, AMERICANS FELT EMBARRASSED THAT THE U.S. WAS THE RUNNER-UP TO THE SOVIETS IN THE SPACE RACE. SO PRESIDENT JOHN F. KENNEDY ISSUED A CHALLENGE THAT TRULY "LAUNCHED" THE U.S. SPACE PROGRAM.

MAY 25, 1961

I BELIEVE THAT THIS NATION SHOULD COMMIT ITSELF TO ACHIEVING THE GOAL, BEFORE THIS DECADE IS OUT, OF LANDING A MAN ON THE MOON AND RETURNING HIM SAFELY TO THE EARTH.

I WAS IN THIS EXACT SPOT FOR A SPEECH GIVEN BY PRESIDENT JAMES K. POLK IN 1848!

IN NO TIME, THE TOP U.S. PILOTS WERE TRAINING FOR THE DIFFICULTIES OF SPACE FLIGHT AND ITS EFFECT ON THE HUMAN BODY. IN ONE SUCH TEST, THE ASTRONAUTS WERE SPUN AT HIGH SPEEDS TO INCREASE THE PRESSURE ON THEIR BODIES. NOT EVERYONE PASSED THE TEST!

WHO LET HIM ON THIS THING ANYWAY?

HE SAYS HE'S FROM THE FUTURE, BOSS!

IN NASA'S NEXT GREAT ACHIEVEMENT, JOHN GLENN BECAME THE FIRST AMERICAN TO ORBIT EARTH, CIRCLING THE PLANET THREE TIMES IN 4 HOURS, 55 MINUTES, AND 23 SECONDS IN HIS *FRIENDSHIP 7* SPACECRAFT.

FEBRUARY 20, 1962

THIS IS A ONCE-IN-A-LIFETIME EXPERIENCE!

ACTUALLY, IN YOUR CASE, IT'S A TWICE-IN-A-LIFETIME EXPERIENCE!

FACT BOX In 1998, at the age of 77, Glenn— who had served 24 years as a U.S. senator— returned to space for a 9-day space shuttle mission.

ALL THESE ACCOMPLISHMENTS WERE LEADING UP TO A CRISP, CLEAR MORNING IN FLORIDA, WHEN ASTRONAUTS NEIL ARMSTRONG, EDWIN "BUZZ" ALDRIN, AND MICHAEL COLLINS BLASTED OFF IN THEIR SPACESHIP, *APOLLO 11.*

JULY 16, 1969, CAPE KENNEDY, FLORIDA. 9:32 A.M.

LIFTOFF! WE HAVE LIFTOFF! THIRTY-TWO MINUTES PAST THE HOUR. LIFTOFF ON *APOLLO 11!*

COULD YOU HAVE THEM DO THAT AGAIN? MY CAMERA FLASH DIDN'T GO OFF.

SOMEBODY GET THIS FUTURE-GUY OUTTA HERE!

FOUR DAYS LATER, AS MORE THAN HALF A BILLION PEOPLE WORLDWIDE WATCHED ON TELEVISION, NEIL ARMSTRONG BECAME THE FIRST HUMAN BEING TO SET FOOT ON THE MOON.

THAT'S ONE SMALL STEP FOR MAN, ONE GIANT LEAP FOR MANKIND.

JULY 20, 1969, 10:56 P.M. EASTERN TIME. THE MOON

THE *APOLLO II* MISSION FULFILLED PRESIDENT KENNEDY'S GOAL OF PUTTING A MAN ON THE MOON BY THE END OF THE 1960S. THE SPACE PROGRAM GAVE US NEW TECHNOLOGIES TO USE ON EARTH. BUT MOST IMPORTANT, THE MOON LANDING SHOWED US IT WAS POSSIBLE TO DREAM BIG AND EVEN REACH THE STARS.

NOW THAT'S WHAT I CALL *OUT OF THIS WORLD!*

SCOOTER'S QUICK QUIZ

1. What was the name of the Soviet Union's first space satellite?

2. What was America's first manned achievement in space?

3. Why do you think President Kennedy made the challenge he did to the U.S. space program?

4. Research NASA's accomplishments in space since 1969. List five missions and describe what the astronauts achieved in each.

5. In the future it may be possible for ordinary people—not just trained astronauts—to travel in space. Would you do this if you had the chance? What would you want to do once you got there?

IN THE 1980s AND 1990s, COMPUTER NETWORKS BECAME BIGGER AND BIGGER. IN 1991, A BRITISH SCIENTIST NAMED TIM BERNERS-LEE LINKED TOGETHER THESE NETWORKS TO INVENT THE **WORLD WIDE WEB.** SURFING THE INTERNET, SENDING E-MAIL, AND INSTANT MESSAGING BECAME A NATURAL PART OF AMERICAN LIFE. BY 2000, 42 OUT OF 100 U.S. HOMES HAD INTERNET ACCESS, AND THE NUMBER CONTINUES TO GROW AND GROW...

HEY, A DOOHICKEY! I HAD ONE IN MY POCKET ALL ALONG!

COMPUTERS ARE CONTINUALLY GETTING FASTER, SMALLER, AND SMARTER. SCIENTISTS ARE ALREADY WORKING ON THE NEXT CHALLENGE: CREATING COMPUTERS THAT CAN "THINK" LIKE HUMANS DO. AND WAIT 'TIL YOU SEE WHAT HAPPENS IN THE YEAR 3016! BUT THAT'S ANOTHER STORY FOR ANOTHER TIME. OH WELL, I'D BETTER GET HOME. I'LL SEE YOU IN THE FUTURE!

SCOOTER'S QUICK QUIZ

1. What was the name of the first high-speed computer that was so big it took up an entire room?

2. What two inventions allowed computers to become faster and smaller?

3. What does it mean for two computers to be networked?

4. Steve Wozniak and Steve Jobs are not the only two American computer giants. Research and describe the contributions of Bill Gates and Paul Allen. What other Americans made major strides in the field of computers?

5. How do you and your family use computers now? Can you imagine how you might use computers 10 years from now? Fifty years from now?

HISTORICAL WHO'S WHO

John Adams (1735–1826): *second President of the United States, 1797–1801*

Samuel Adams (1722–1803): *American Revolutionary patriot*

Jane Addams (1860–1935): *Chicago-based social reformer*

Madeleine Albright (1937–): *first female U.S. Secretary of State*

Edwin "Buzz" Aldrin (1930–): *astronaut, second person to walk on the moon*

Susan B. Anthony (1820–1906): *suffragist and women's rights advocate*

Neil Armstrong (1930–): *astronaut, first person to walk on the moon*

Crispus Attucks (1723?–1770): *African American killed in the Boston Massacre*

Tim Berners-Lee (1955–): *British inventor of the World Wide Web*

Amelia Bloomer (1818–1894): *suffragist and advocate for less restrictive women's clothing*

Sam Brannan (1819–1889): *colorful entrepreneur of the Gold Rush*

Harry Burn (1895–1977): *Tennessee state assemblyman who cast the deciding vote for ratification of the 19th Amendment*

Hattie Wyatt Caraway (1878–1950): *first woman elected U.S. senator, from Arkansas*

Jean-Baptiste Charbonneau (1805–1866): *son of Sacagawea and Toussaint Charbonneau*

Toussaint Charbonneau (1758?–1843?): *French-Canadian fur trader and husband of Sacagawea*

William Clark (1770–1838): *famed explorer with Meriwether Lewis*

Michael Collins (1930–): *command module pilot on* Apollo 11 *flight to the moon*

William Dawes (1745–1799): *patriot and fellow rider with Paul Revere*

Geraldine Ferraro (1935–): *first female vice-presidential candidate, 1984*

Henry Ford (1863–1947): *automobile manufacturer*

Benjamin Franklin (1706–1790): *statesman, diplomat, author, and scientist*

Betty Friedan (1921–): *feminist author and founder of National Organization for Women*

Yuri Gagarin (1934–1968): *Soviet cosmonaut, first man in space*

King George III (1738–1820): *British monarch, 1760–1820; ruled during American Revolution*

Ruth Bader Ginsburg (1933–): *second female Supreme Court justice*

John Glenn (1921–): *astronaut and U.S. senator, first American to orbit in space*

Ella Grasso (1919–1981): *first woman elected governor, of Connecticut*

Alexander Hamilton (1755–1804): *patriot and statesman, first Secretary of the U.S. Treasury*

John Hancock (1737–1793): *patriot famed for his prominent signature on the Declaration of Independence*

John Jay (1745–1829): *patriot and statesman, first justice of the Supreme Court*

Thomas Jefferson (1743–1826): *third President of the United States, 1801–1809; also author, scientist, educator, and architect; one of the authors of the Declaration of Independence*

Steve Jobs (1955–): *cofounder of Apple computer company*

John F. Kennedy (1917–1963): *35th President of the United States, 1961–63, and member of a prominent American political family*

Laika (?–1957): *Soviet dog, first living creature in space*

John Larkin (17?–18?): *deacon from Charlestown, Massachusetts, who loaned a horse to Paul Revere for the Midnight Ride*

Meriwether Lewis (1774–1809): *famed explorer with William Clark*

Robert Livingston (1746–1813): *patriot who helped write the Declaration of Independence; later was sent to France to negotiate the Louisiana Purchase*

James Madison (1751–1836): *fourth President of the United States, 1809–1817; was primary author of the U.S. Constitution*

James Marshall (1810–1885): *credited with first discovery of gold in the Gold Rush*

Massasoit (1580?–1661): *New England Native American leader*

John Mauchly (1907–1980): *computer pioneer and one of the inventors of Electronic Numerical Integrator and Computer (ENIAC)*

Lucretia Mott (1793–1880): *suffragist and women's rights advocate*

Sandra Day O'Connor (1930–): *first female Supreme Court justice*

Rosa Parks (1913–): *hero of the Civil Rights movement*

James K. Polk (1795–1849): *11th President of the United States, 1845–1849*

Samuel Prescott (1751–1777): *doctor, patriot, and fellow rider with Paul Revere*

Jeannette Rankin (1880–1973): *feminist, activist, and first woman elected to the U.S. House of Representatives, from Montana*

Janet Reno (1938–): *first female U.S. Attorney General*

Paul Revere (1735–1818): *silversmith and patriot who made the famous Midnight Ride*

Jacob Riis (1849–1914): *photographer and social reformer*

Eleanor Roosevelt (1884–1962): *First Lady to Franklin Delano Roosevelt; also author and diplomat*

Sacagawea (1786?–1812): *Native American guide and interpreter for Lewis and Clark*

Samoset (1590?–1653?): *Native American chief who assisted the Plymouth Pilgrims*

Seaman (early 1800s): *Newfoundland dog owned by Meriwether Lewis*

Alan Shepard (1923–1998): *astronaut, first American in space*

Roger Sherman (1721–1793): *patriot who helped write the Declaration of Independence*

Squanto (?–1622): *Native American friend of Plymouth Pilgrims*

Elizabeth Cady Stanton (1815–1902): *suffragist and women's rights advocate*

Levi Strauss (1829–1902): *famed denim-pants manufacturer*

John Sutter (1803–1880): *owner of the California mill where gold was discovered*

Charles Townshend (1725–1767): *British finance minister who levied taxes on the colonies*

Sojourner Truth (1797–1883): *born into slavery as Isabella Baumfree; abolitionist and women's rights advocate*

George Washington (1732–1799): *first President of the United States, 1789–1797; general of the Continental Army and hero of the Revolutionary War*

Steve Wozniak (1950–): *cofounder of Apple computer company*

Konrad Zuse (1910–1995): *German inventor of the first programmable digital computer*

ANSWER KEY

The Pilgrims of Plymouth

1. The "Mayflower Compact" was a document signed by the Pilgrims, who agreed to work together under a shared set of rules.
2. The Pilgrims left no historical record of landing on a famous rock. The Plymouth Rock that sits in Plymouth, Massachusetts, today is a symbolic landing site.
3. Samoset
4. William Bradford was the first governor of the Plymouth colony; he served 30 years and wrote a famous history of the colony. Myles Standish was a professional soldier and the colony's military advisor.
5. Answers will vary. Thanksgiving was not always a national holiday. In October 1777, the 13 colonies first observed Thanksgiving at the same time. In 1789, George Washington first declared Thanksgiving a holiday. By the mid-1800s, many Americans celebrated Thanksgiving as a state holiday. Writer Sarah J. Hale began to push for a true national holiday and discussed the idea with President Lincoln during the Civil War. In 1863, Lincoln delivered the Thanksgiving Proclamation, declaring the last Thursday in November a day of thanksgiving. In 1939, 1940, and 1941 President Franklin D. Roosevelt proclaimed Thanksgiving the third Thursday in November. However, in 1941 Congress decided that Thanksgiving should fall on the fourth Thursday of November, where we celebrate it today.

The Boston Tea Party

1. The British instituted taxes in the colonies to raise money after the French and Indian War. The Stamp Act taxed all printed matter. The Townshend Acts taxed paper, paint, glass, and tea.
2. The Sons of Liberty
3. Through the Tea Act, the King allowed the British East India Tea Company to sell tea at very low prices. Tea merchants in the colonies couldn't compete and were going out of business.
4. A boycott is the act of abstaining from using, buying, or dealing with an organization to express protest. Students can research other boycotts such as the Montgomery bus boycott (1956) during the fight for Civil Rights; the 1980 Olympic boycott, in which the U.S. protested the Soviet Union's invasion of Afghanistan; and the Irish peasants' protesting the policies of the British land agent Charles Cunningham Boycott—the world's first true boycott!
5. Answers will vary. In a democratic society, citizens have a say in matters of government. In the U.S. Congress, our views are voiced by senators and representatives from our state and local district.

Midnight Ride of Paul Revere!

1. Lanterns in the Old North Church signaled "one if by land, two if by sea."
2. Revere had to warn John Hancock and Samuel Adams that they were in danger.
3. William Dawes and Samuel Prescott
4. Revere had to cross the Charles River.
5. In Longfellow's poem, Revere makes the entire ride alone. There is no mention of his arrest and release by the British.

More specifically, it was midnight when he got to Lexington, not 1 A.M. as Longfellow writes; and Samuel Prescott continued the ride to Concord, not Revere.

The Shocking Life of Benjamin Franklin

1. He wanted to prove that electricity and lightning were the same thing. He hoped that lightning would strike the metal tip of his kite.
2. Ben Franklin, Thomas Jefferson, John Adams, Roger Sherman, and Robert Livingston
3. *Poor Richard's Almanack*
4. Answers will vary. Some additional sayings might include "An ounce of prevention is worth a pound of cure" (attend to matters before they become a big problem); "To err is human, to repent divine; to persist devilish" (more commonly paraphrased as "To err is human, to forgive divine," suggests that everyone makes mistakes, but the best people can forgive); "We must all hang together, or assuredly we shall all hang separately" (if the colonies did not unite, the British would prevail); and "Fish and visitors stink after three days" (don't overstay your welcome!).
5. Alexander Hamilton, who appears on the $10 bill, was the first Secretary of the U.S. Treasury and a major author of the Federalist papers. (See "The Constitution and the Bill of Rights" comic.)

The Constitution and the Bill of Rights

1. The Articles of Confederation
2. James Madison
3. In a system of checks and balances, no one branch of government has more power than the others. The branches check each others' work, so the power is balanced. For example, the president can veto the Congress; courts test the constitutionality of Congress's laws; and Congress can override the president's veto.
4. Big states, such as Virginia, wanted more say in government because they had greater populations. Small states such as New Jersey believed each state should have equal say in the government. The Great Compromise allowed both conditions to be met in a single Congress. The Senate was roughly modeled on the British Parliament's House of Lords, and the House of Representatives was roughly modeled on Parliament's House of Commons.
5. Answers will vary. Some of the additional amendments have dealt with limiting presidential terms, granting the right to vote to women and African Americans, prohibition of slavery, and the establishment of income tax.

The Lewis & Clark Expedition

1. The Louisiana Territory
2. The Corps of Discovery
3. The Indians they met let them have a place to stay for the winter, acted as interpreters, lent them horses, and helped them make canoes.
4. President Jefferson asked them to map the new lands, study plants and animals, and befriend any native people they encountered. Along the way, Clark drew the first accurate maps of many American rivers and mountains. In his journal, Lewis described 178 plants and 122 animals no scientist had ever seen. And together they made friends with the Missouris, the Omahas, and the Yankton Sioux Indians.

5. Answers will vary. Students would probably want to bring along tools to gather and prepare food, protection against the elements, maps, and a mode of transportation.

California Gold Rush!

1. The big movement west in search of gold began in 1849.
2. James K. Polk, the 11th U.S. President
3. Iron pyrite, or "fool's gold," looks like gold but has little real value. It can easily be broken with a hammer.
4. Some would-be miners sailed to California around the coast of South America, which could take up to six months. Later, others took a "shortcut" through Panama, which was still difficult, as the Panama Canal was not built until 1914.
5. Answers will vary.

The Story of America's Immigrants

1. Ellis Island
2. France gave the Statue of Liberty to the United States to celebrate our Centennial (100th birthday). Accept a variety of answers for what the statue represents. To the immigrants, it was a welcoming symbol of America's hope and freedom.
3. Answers will vary. As the saying goes, "A picture is worth a thousand words." Riis's photos of poor living conditions in the ghettos made the immigrants' plight more real to anyone who saw the photos with their own eyes.
4. Answers will vary. Students wishing to research their family's connection to Ellis Island may use this Web site: www.ellisisland.org
5. Answers will vary. America's diversity has taught our nation to be tolerant and accepting of all ethnicities and religions. The best ideas from many nations have enriched America's unique cultural heritage and its economy.

Henry Ford and the Assembly Line

1. The Quadricycle
2. The Model A and the Model T. Each of Ford's successive car designs was named after the next letter in the alphabet.
3. Ford wanted to build the cheapest car possible in the least amount of time.
4. Anti-Semitism is discrimination, anger, or prejudice against Jews. Henry Ford's anti-Semitism has hurt his historical image. During World War II, Adolf Hitler, leader of Nazi Germany, led a ruthless military campaign, which resulted in the death of 6 million Jews.
5. Answers will vary. Some moments could include the invention of the gas engine in 1885, Gottlieb Daimler's first four-wheeled motorcar, the first car sold in the U.S. by the Duryea brothers—or the advent of the sports car after World War II.

The Fight for Women's Rights

1. The first Women's Rights Convention, held in Seneca Falls, New York, was organized by Elizabeth Cady Stanton, Lucretia Mott, and others.
2. Truth explains that if slaves should be free, then all women should also be free.
3. Anthony voted to draw attention to the cause of women's suffrage.
4. Answers will vary. The historic figures include Elizabeth Cady Stanton, Lucretia Mott, Sojourner Truth, Amelia Bloomer, Susan B. Anthony, Jeannette Rankin, and all the women mentioned in the final page of the comic. Students may be particularly interested in the life of Jeannette Rankin, whose career in politics stretched from the suffrage years to her prominent opposition of U.S. involvement in World War I, World War II, and the Vietnam War.
5. The Equal Rights Amendment (ERA) says that state or national law shall not discriminate against any American on account of their gender. Suffragist Alice Paul wrote the ERA in 1921, and it was debated in Congress each year from 1923 to 1982. In 1972, Congress passed the amendment, but it was ratified by only 35 states—not the necessary 38—prior to its July 1982 deadline. (See "The Constitution and the Bill of Rights" comic for ratification of amendments.) American women continue to fight for fair pay for equal work, maternity leave, workplace day care, health care, and reproductive rights.

America's Race to the Moon

1. *Sputnik*
2. Astronaut Alan Shepard's 15-minute flight in 1961
3. Answers will vary. In general, Kennedy saw American achievement in space as an extension of the Cold War between the United States and the Soviet Union.
4. Answers will vary. Students might include *Skylab*, the *Apollo-Soyuz* Test Project, the space shuttle, the Hubble Space Telescope, and the International Space Station.
5. Answers will vary. Student may want to research the experiences of Dennis Tito and Lance Bass (of *NSYNC), two American civilians who received training in the Russian space program.

Computers and the Internet

1. ENIAC (Electronic Numerical Integrator and Computer)
2. Transistors and integrated circuits (chips)
3. Networked computers are linked to each other and can share data.
4. Answers will vary. Bill Gates and Paul Allen are the cofounders of Microsoft, the world's biggest software company. Other individuals your students may wish to research include Ray Tomlinson, Grace Hopper, Vint Cerf, Jack Kilby, Robert Noyce, and Gordon Moore.
5. Answers will vary. Today, computers and the Internet are often used for research, entertainment, shopping, and banking. In years to come, your students' guesses are as good as ours—or better! Encourage creative responses.